Why?

There are so many times we have to

wonder why.

To be surprised,
to wonder,
is to begin
to understand.

José Ortega Y Gasset

Why can't the answers be more plain?

Why can't the answers be more plain?

Why or pain?

Joy or pain?

Success or failure?

Why are there things we can't explain?

It is better to ask
some of the questions
than to know
all of the answers.

James Thurber

Does everything happen for a reason?

Sometimes we do a thing in order to find out the reason for it. Sometimes our actions are questions not answers.

John Le Carré

Do two people meet by accident, or is it meant to be?

...there can be no accidents or loose ends, nothing whatever of which we can safely use the word "merely"

C. S. Lewis

Are some people simply lucky?

If it's true, it's plain to see
that luck and accidents
are not as simple
as they seem to be.

*It is a great piece of skill to know
how to guide your luck
even while waiting for it.*

Baltasar Gracián

Maybe
everything happens
for a reason.

*Trust your instinct to the end,
though you can render no reason.*

Ralph Waldo Emerson

We may try,
but there are
powers
that we simply
can't deny.

I believe it
because it is
unbelievable.

Tertullian

When

we sometimes receive...

while some receive...

some sacrifice...

Misfortune
wandering the same track
lights now upon one
and now upon another.

Aeschylus

we sometimes struggle to believe...

while others grieve...

some rejoice...

...that everything

happens for a reason.

The heart has its reasons
which reason knows nothing of.

Blaise Pascal

Some say
it's fate.

*I do not believe
in a fate that
falls on men
however they act;
but I do believe
in a fate that
falls on them
unless they act.*

G. K. Chesterton

Some say
coincidence.

Some say
they're both
the same.

Something good
we should be
grateful for,

We cannot freely and wisely
choose the right way for ourselves
unless we know both good and evil.

Helen Keller

or something bad
to blame.

Learn
to get in touch
with the silence
within yourself
and know that
everything in this life
has a purpose.

Elisabeth Kubler-Ross

Or known by any other name...

...Or known God's guiding hand...

God's guiding hand...

A master plan...

Everything happens for a reason.

It is that purpose in the universe
that always works

I am here for a purpose,
and that purpose
is to grow into a mountain,

for good, even though the world won't always turn the way we wish it would.

not shrink to a grain of sand. Og Mandino

And though we cannot understand it,

still,

somehow,

Between
Our birth and death
we may touch understanding
As a moth brushes a window
with its wing.

Christopher Fry

it's understood...

What I have
in my heart
must come out;

Everything
happens
for a reason.

that is the reason
why I compose.

Ludwig van Beethoven

invisible decision with each step along the way. Life has given us the freedom to make choices every day—one

When you have to
make a choice
and don't make it;
that in itself
is a choice.

William James

Two roads diverged in a wood, and I —
I took the one less traveled by,
And that has made all the difference.

Robert Frost

And with each choice, a brand new pathway.

Where it leads to... who can say?

...but
everything
happens
for a reason.

There is
no reason
not to follow
your heart.

Steve Jobs

Times we do the things we choose, and times we do the things we must. There are times we change our lives, and there

...are times life changes us.

Change is the law of life.
And those who look
only to the past or the present
are certain to miss the future.

John F. Kennedy

There are times
we understand,

and times
we simply
have to trust

*Faith is to believe
what you do not yet see;
the reward for this faith
is to see what you believe.*

St. Augustine

that everything happens
for a reason.

There is a reason why a grain of sand can make a perfect pearl.

I believe God made me for a purpose,
but he also made me fast.
And when I run, I feel His pleasure.

Eric Liddel

There is a reason you were made, a man or woman, boy or girl.

There is a reason
you are reading this.

Your life
has changed the world.

Everything
happens
for a reason.

A million miracles are waiting to be found. Look all around.

To me every hour
of the light and dark
is a miracle,
Every cubic inch of space
is a miracle.

Walt Whitman

if we are willing
to believe

and we have dreams
we can achieve,

We still have time
before we leave,

that everything happens

for a reason.

Nothing happens
unless first a dream.

Carl Sandburg

We will see it, if we look to find a reason to believe. We will see it, if we look to find a reason to believe.

*Everything possible to be believed
is an image of truth.*

William Blake

Everything happens

for a reason.

for Becky,
for a million reasons

Library of Congress Cataloging-in-Publication Data

Hanson, Warren.
  Everything happens for a reason / written and illustrated by
  Warren Hanson.
     p. cm.
  ISBN-13: 978-0-931674-85-3 (hardcover : alk. paper)
  ISBN-10: 0-931674-85-9 (hardcover : alk. paper) 1. Life change
  events--Psychological aspects. 2. Meaning (Psychology)
  3. Conduct of life. I. Title.
  BF637.L53.H376 2009
  158.1--dc22   2009021739

TRISTAN Publishing, Inc.
2355 Louisiana Avenue North
Golden Valley, MN 55427

Please visit us at:
www.tristanpublishing.com